www.PaulineRitchieMoore.com

This book is dedicated to each and every person who has made a conscious effort to wake up to their purpose in life! You have chosen wisely and abundantly-LIFT UP YOUR HEADS AND THRIVE ABUNDANTLY!!

Ritchie Publishing

350 East Six Forks Road, Suite 150 – #30932

Raleigh, NC 27622

Dedications and Thanks

It is with unimaginable gratitude that I take a moment to say "THANK YOU" from the bottom of my heart, first to the Source Of All Creation (God) for showing me that I am a reflection of The One Who Has Dominion Over All That Is.

Next, I would like to thank my parents Bishop Donald and First Lady Lucille Ritchie (2006) for without your lives as examples of fearlessness, I would not be who I am today.

An eternal "THANK YOU" to my husband, Raymond L. Moore, also known as "The Man" for his unconditional love for me. Your love makes me greater!

To my brother Randy Ritchie, also known as "The Sage", your support, wisdom and purpose has contributed immeasurably to this writing. I look forward to reading your upcoming publications for they will offer even more thought provoking insight into the heart of all that is wise and true.

To my brother Mark Ritchie, also known as "The Tycoon", your encouragement and brain power are the fuel for greatness as is evident in your daily life. You are my twin!

To my *égaux en intelligence*, Walter "Trace" Parham, you continue to provide the intellect, depth perception, and antithetical perspective that is so valuable to great writing without fear of offending my tough exterior. Thank you. You are priceless!

Table Of Contents

CHAPTER 10

CHAPTER 11

CHAPTER 12

CHAPTER 13

Right Before the SHIFT Happens, This Happens...

Like many of you, I sat in churches of all denominations for many years beginning at birth. And while I saw many life affirming acts of love in some of the churches, I also witnessed many superfluous religious rituals, services and sermons in each denomination including Churches of God In Christ (C.O.G.I.C), Pentecostal Assemblies of the World (P.A.W.), Apostolic Overcoming Holiness (A.O.H) churches, Baptist churches, Centers For Spiritual Living (C.S.L.) and even nondenominational churches among others. And of course I could have continued attending these ceremonial gatherings in this way until I expired. I could have stayed on a never ending carousel attending service after service, hearing sermon after sermon and serving on boards and committees forever. But many of us who have been serving in these capacities since day one have begun experiencing within us a nagging inner discomfort due to unaddressed "soul" questions which has eventually grown into an insatiably deep dissatisfaction with unrealized potential, undesirable living conditions, mediocrity, and a downright unhappiness with the current state of things in our spiritual lives, our churches, our ministers, and ultimately our faith. This has not changed in decades and in most of our lives, it has gotten worse. And with this spiritual dissatisfaction, our seeking began for we knew within us that there was more. However, when we are first prompted to seek a higher knowing, there emerges from our core a fear. What is this fear? What causes it? This fear is due to our classic conditioning against the need to question our strongest core beliefs...beliefs that were drilled into us by repetition, by environment, by family, and by association. We were conditioned to know these beliefs as "THE ONLY TRUTH" and we were, quite frankly, scared to question them for fear of rejection, claims of heresy, demon possession, or worst of all, threats that we were listening to the devil and on our way to hell. This is a prime example of dogmatism and intentional fear-based programming by those with their own personal agenda for our lives. How scary! But this dogmatic rhetoric is not from a God of eternal, unconditional love but from humans who needed our fear to control us. God is not a God who wants our servitude out of fear, for this fear would lead us to flee at the first opportunity to escape, as many of us did. This fear was ingrained so deeply into us that after a while, no one had to say a word to us about our questions, for we would rebuke ourselves before a word was ever uttered against those core beliefs. In our minds, we experienced such cognitive dissonance about questioning deeper and wanting to know more beyond what we were told that we prayed that the urge to question would go away and blind faith would return. But then we grew and purpose began to emerge and God began to reveal in us the longing, the boldness to dare to go deeper, higher, further. And so our journey began. We first start the journey by looking at those around us, in our immediate vicinity. We are looking at our parents, our teachers, our Pastors and their wives, our choir members, and even our coworkers. And while many of the Pastors, preachers, ministers, laypeople, friends and family around us are wonderful, good hearted, spiritually sound beings, we still begin to ask, to question, to test the faith hoping to find the Light we seek. Unfortunately, among the sheep we always find wolves in sheep's clothing. It is to the wolves that we are speaking here. As we question in our earnest seeking, some sheep around us try and they have good intentions, but it is more of the same. More quoting selected scriptures, more clichés, more words without the intimate personal one-on-one experience of God, more rituals and empty actions. Some can only recite what their parents told them, only what they have heard and are determined to believe and perpetuate because they know nothing more. The wolves don't even care to try because they never did believe in anything deeper than the outward show of "holiness" on demand and so they turn to harsh judgment of us. And then there are the bigger wolves who hope for the opportunity to exploit our seeking. They lie in wait and watch as they see the need to know arising. They expect it. They say all of the right words, use all of the right terms and perform all of the right rituals to bait and to coax the seeker to come to them with their longing to know more. And then they strike! They pull you aside, away from outside noise (but preferably away from that inner voice of God which is impossible to do) and begin to teach you what they feel is suitable for you to know....about giving of your time to their programs, your money to their causes, your skills and resources to further their agendas and ministries. Yes, giving is essential, but why are you giving when your search has not been satisfied but has been discouraged? Are you giving freely or paying in vain hoping for that deep soul searching to be satisfied? But the TRUE AND LIVING GOD IN YOU just keeps prompting you to seek, to search deeper in hopes that you will acknowledge His presence and live by it. But alas, because of contact with wolves, you are barely hopeful but hopeful nonetheless. Your hope lies in the very thought of a possible light at the end of the "hole in your soul" tunnel, however against your better judgment, against the God in you, you acquiesce and settle for the catch-all phrase, "just have faith" which is used by wolves to avoid answering the deepest soul questions. You tell yourself that having blind faith is what has been done for years so it must be right. Most of the people you know do it and they seem "normal" so it must be right. You tell yourself, "That many people can't be wrong, can they?" You accept their instructions reluctantly and although you want to protest because the longing has not been thoroughly addressed, you don't. They say, "We believe it so it must be right". And so, the cycle continues of ritualistic servitude and there you remain seeking, semi awake yet unfulfilled for months, years, and for some, a lifetime. For those who feel the urgent prompting of their purpose and destiny, this is not enough for them and after a very short period of time the need for more overtakes them yet again. And as always, the Source Of All Creation inside of them sends unmistakable messages to confirm this by (a) irrefutable evidence placed in the soul and consciousness directly from God that does not agree with what has been repeated to them by many for years, (b) counter feelings (uncomfortable with what they have been told) that confirm the aforementioned evidence, (c) personal interactions with those living the status quo that usually end in a manner that might from the naked eye appear to be negative, however, later it is rightly understood as a necessity for growth and (d) situations and circumstances that seem to synchronize their outward situation with their divine purpose. And having not reached a higher consciousness comfort level in their current state, they spend the next few years going from church to church, from temple to temple, from group to group, from preacher to preacher and guru to guru with integral stints of time completely away from church, spirituality and religion altogether. They sit at home in frustration. All with that irritating question screaming over and over in their minds, "Is there more? THERE HAS TO BE MORE!". Eventually, they come to understand that their search has been tantamount to looking for love in all the wrong places. In many, many cases, YOU may have found yourself stagnant and bitter while some have turned away from hope altogether without ever knowing that there is so much more. Having retreated from religion, you were riddled with guilt and shame. But among the many who remained in the shadows of shame arose a fearless few who followed that inner knowing that there IS a true "God-experience" that far outweighs the fear of condemnation for interrogating core beliefs in favor of real involvement with God. Although some gave in and returned to the religion of their past out of guilt or obligation or ignorance of something greater, they too have looked in the mirror of life and asked, "How have these religious and philosophical beliefs been working for me?" If your beliefs have not been working at 100%, then are you willing...DO YOU DARE to set them aside for a moment and seek anew? Think for a moment. Are you Prosperous? Abundant? Alive? Productive? Resourceful? Loving? Giving? At Peace? Peaceful? Happy and Living on

Purpose? If the answer is yes, then read on so that the momentum to share your purpose with others takes off! However, if even one of these attributes is missing from your life, then be ready to begin again, to seek and you shall find. This is the promise, it is a Universal law...

~~~~~~

First Things First

No Preachers, No Gurus, Just God

When this book was given to me by my Creator, my first human inclination was fear, for I knew this message would generate everything from raised eyebrows to an outright fight from those who are not interested in the growth and enlightenment of themselves, the people in their lives and those under their guidance. However, a half second of my fear quickly turned into complete faith and love as God my Source reminded me of why this message was given to me and that the fight against it was not mine. The purpose of this book is not to tear down any sincere preacher, guru, imam, spiritual leader, minister, or follower but just the opposite. The purpose of this book is to reshape and reform our perception of those positions into a more expanded, right-sized, more open, more inclusive, more realistic, more loving, more divine interpretation of what we should be as the Voice Of God. Now it is expected that what you read here will stretch you to new places that will be uncomfortable but let's face it, if you remain comfortable nothing will change and nothing will get better. Things will remain as they are currently or God forbid get worse. It is time now to release old interpretations and ideas to make room for new fresh life! You already know that the next level lies well outside of your comfort zone so prepare to be uncomfortable as you move into that next level. It will undoubtedly be a bit scary, for your long held beliefs will be challenged. You will be prompted to expand beyond what you and those around you have been conditioned to accept and believe. You may even be ostracized or even persecuted by those you love. But, fear not for it is no coincidence that you have received this book and dare to read it all of the way through for here is the crux of the matter regarding fear. Humans tend to fear what they don't understand and fear leads to "fight or flight"...and let me tell you that upon being given a glimpse into my purpose, I had done enough of both. Yes, it has been a fight from the moment of enlightenment for me, not only with inner, long held, unquestioned beliefs passed over to me, but from the religious community in particular, and some who haven't been fair with their fight. But anytime change is to come, it will always be met with fight by the status quo. **There are those who are so deeply rooted in religion that they will read each word of this book and judge it with so closed a mind that they won't be able to finish it.** They will be poised to fight without ever understanding the growth possibilities in it, if not for themselves, for those around them. But we cannot be afraid of the fight for it is not ours. There are two fights in progress when change is imminent- the fight inside of ourselves and the fight from those around us. Once we arrest the fight within us with knowledge and a true, direct, one-on-one experience with the God in us, the fight from others is already won. The word to me from The Source of All Creation was this: Don't fight those who are afraid of change for they have mastered the fight on their level and they never fight fair, however, they lack the ability to rise above their current level so again, DON'T FIGHT THEM, TRANSCEND THEM and you will win every time. They can go lower, but they cannot go higher or they would have instead of resorting to words and actions less befitting the God in them. And so, it is with peace, love and faith that these words come to you to encourage you to expansion….

Why Write A Book That Will Offend?

In order to be offended by something, you first have to sense that you are being attacked. Upon further examination, you will note that it is not you personally who is being attacked (wolves are the exception) but you might feel that a concept that you have believed since as far back as you can remember is being called into question. Yes, they are being called into question but not to attack or wage war but to cause growth and expansion. If you feel your beliefs are being attacked, then set your underlying fear aside and ask yourself why? Offense is fear based. What are you afraid of? If your lifelong beliefs are what we all hope that they should be then they will stand the test of time easily. If not, then you deserve growth and expansion in the very area of offense. Do not be afraid as your current definition of God may change from its human-like limitations to the "everything, everywhere, all powerful, applicable-to-life-right-now Force" but isn't that how it should be? *"Well, God is already all of that to me,"* you say. Then your life is full, purposeful, joyful, helpful, whole, prosperous, abundant, and lacking nothing? If so, then read further for possible expansion. If not, then you too should read on for your life will surely be changed. But if you read on and experience the fear of offense, then it is the opinion of this writer that your fear will be due to your severely underrated definition of who you are for fear cannot dwell in the same temple with Faith. Are you afraid that your definition of you will be uplifted to its rightful place? Your life is what it is because of your thinking. If you keep thinking what you are thinking then you will keep manifesting the very same outcome. Now that can be a great thing if your thinking is great, powerful and abundant. You will know what you think by looking around you. During this wonderful and amazing time of great awakening, those who have held beliefs that were longstanding in institutions, cultures, communities, and among friends are being prompted to look deeper, to open up more, to dialogue and to understand, to build on and accept a new thought process that serves to bring us into full enlightenment, into higher consciousness, into the full knowledge of self as the image of God that Genesis 1:27 speaks of (So God created man in his *own* image, in the image of God created he him; male and female created he them). Religious leaders these days are seeking a new truth just as diligently as their congregations are, knowing that the new framework for higher consciousness is one of Creator-inspired ideas, not rules, regulations or dogma. The fear of offending those who don't want growth and change WILL NOT stop the growth and change...it will only cause the message to come from a source/vessel that is not willing to allow fear to impede growth and change or stop their purpose. The new framework is of individuals seeking to be more highly evolved and more directly connected to the Source, and not groups, denominations, or cliques. This new framework of people will have NOTHING AND NO ONE between God and themselves and exist to be directly connected to the Source for their journey will dictate that they be. They...WE consider ourselves an appendage of God as well as a vessel that houses God who is the Source of All Creation, The Creator of Everything, The God of the Universe (His voice can be heard throughout the Universe in every form fathomable and unfathomable). They have and will continue to come to understand that their direct connection will automatically connect them to all others on the planet since the Source is within all and is all. No one will be excluded, no one left out regardless of their past, present, or any other human borders. And so to the question of writing a book that might offend I say, it's time. It's time to go to the next level and although offending others is far from the intent of the message, offense is inherent in upward mobility by default. If this book has a goal, it is to point the way to the Light within and away from *the fallacy* that says that 1) we the people NEED any one "picture perfect leader" to accept responsibility for our spiritual connection to God or, 2) that a leader should be perfect to lead or 3) that the people cannot lead because they are not "picture perfect". Many religious leaders seem to have run dry of what is needed for their congregations to move to the next level-a new, personal, intimate, individual experiential, real relationship with God that prompts them to pure, sure, confident action in their everyday lives moment-to-moment through love. Many have gone dry, gone Hollywood, gone astray or gone away because they want to grow but are "boxed in" by tradition, ritual, inflexible organizations, and fear. Neale Donald Walsch insists that, "***the supreme irony here is that you have all*** *placed so much importance on the Word of God and so little on the experience (of God). In fact, you place so little value on the experience (of God) that when what you experience of God differs from what you have heard of God, you automatically discard the experience and own the words, when it should be just the other way around"* *from Neale Donald Walsch's Conversation With God - Book 1 pg 4.* Unfortunately, or fortunately, when a man or woman dares to sound the trumpet and tell you what reason denies, he or she becomes the enemy or crazy or a witch or demon possessed or some other villainous entity. Perceived and long held beliefs masquerading as "facts" do not overcome newly understood truth. We are waking up!

(God will be referred to in the male tense for this writing since we as humans need to confine His presence so that it fits nicely in the container of our limited minds. Note that He is not a he or a she...He is Asexual meaning He can reproduce by processes that do not involve the union of individuals or gametes, therefore no male nor female gender is needed for Him to create or recreate, yet He created all things)

Preachers, Gurus And The People

The media blasts so many news docudramas, talk shows and newsfeeds in society that decry the big powerful predatory preachers preying on the poor defenseless weak little lambs for their money and to this I say, HOGWASH! First to address the congregation, who are not prey by any means. Most churchgoers who give of their money, time and talent are educated, intelligent professionals, many of whom are business owners, attorneys, doctors, teachers, analysts, scientists, and other degreed, and learned professionals. Religious leaders and others in authority can do nothing, absolutely nothing, without the cooperation, support, and eager submission of their congregation especially in the current information age that we live in. Many parishioners have long since recused themselves from their own lives and gladly placed blame and responsibility for their failure to launch at the feet of the religious leaders. But that time is past and now EVERYONE must accept responsibility for their own spiritual life choices. Ignorance on the part of the congregation is not at play here...but many parishioners do tend to lean on the crutches of following traditions, failure to accept responsibility for one's spiritual health, easing ones conscience, or buying a position or "ticket" to heaven as a way of justifying the willful ignorance of responsibility where their personal contact with God is concerned. If many a well versed churchgoer insists on saying that "someone (the preacher) keeps doing this to me (taking my money)", they are attempting to absolve themselves of the responsibility to acknowledge the indwelling Spirit, educate themselves, properly distribute their God-given resources, and renew their mind to live their calling.

I remember a time many years ago and prior to my awakening that I would sit in many church services barely able to concentrate on anything that was going on at the time because my mind was racing in a state of worry about my own lack on money. In my mind, I plotted ways to leave the sanctuary right before the financial "offering" because I didn't want to feel the discomfort of the self-allowed pressure of having to put even one dollar in the basket, nor did I want to look like my condition at that time...which was pretty close to broke. Yes, I had been told in many churches that if I gave even my last $20 that it would be multiplied back to me tenfold. But more often than not, the little bit of money that I had was already spoken for by landlords, bill collectors, and more importantly at that time, the gas station that needed to be paid for whatever I filled my tank up with. In most cases, I heard the tenfold thing but when I looked around, it was very clear that some of the money collectors had an abundance of gas in the tanks of their brand new high end vehicles while I worried about whether or not I could even make it to the gas station but make no mistake about it, that was ALL MY OWN FAULT. Why was it my own fault? Because that still, small voice inside that always takes better care of me than anyone else was telling me the entire time what I needed to do but instead of listening, I chose to allow it to be drowned out by the voices of people...people that I was told had the authority to speak into my life over the voice of God in me. I didn't know who I was at that time but it only took a short amount of seeking to realize that the prompting, urging, and motivating that my inner voice had done since as far back as I can remember has worked in my favor without fail, 100% of the time. I only needed to be taught to recognize, acknowledge, allow and accept the leading of this Unlimited Inner God-Source. Had I known then to listen to the Indwelling Spirit within me, I would have taken the little money that I had, sowed it into my purpose and as I lived my calling, provision unto abundance would have been manifested and I would not have had to cringe at the thought of giving or running out of gas or both. But instead, I paid into everyone else's vision for their lives. It was only when I learned God's voice that abundance manifested in my life and allowed me the freedom to live, move, and have my being. But this freedom could only come when I accepted the fact that those outside of me...yes, some of those who asserted authority over me were humans and NO human's words should never take the place of the voice of The Source Of All Creation within each of us.

There is freedom in knowing God's voice and acceptance of it! There is freedom for you and freedom for those you have accepted as leadership who have been unfairly placed on a pedestal between you and your Source. They too deserve to be free to be loving, caring humans who fall and get up without unearned, overemphasized scrutiny of their lives.

There is growth, expansion, love and tolerance in acceptance of your responsibility to be the Light and share the Light that you have gone to church hoping, praying and longing to see in the leadership and others. And most importantly, acceptance contains within it the knowing that you have been and always will be the apple of God's eye and the purpose for His existence! God prefers that you come directly to Him within yourself and not go to outside sources as couriers between you and Him. Why? Because all humans, whether knowingly or unknowingly have the propensity to insert their own versions, tendencies, biases, outlooks, prejudices, beliefs and interpretations into God's words and all things that are spiritual, philosophical or religious in nature. And herein lies the plight of many a follower of religion X, Y, or Z. The things that the minister, guru, orator or reverend might say seems to be right because a scripture was quoted and that speaker's interpretation appeared to match perfectly with the reading...until paradigms about the meanings of those words began to shift and expand, which is the beginning of enlightenment... new meanings, new definitions, new direction and new revelation. Many, many religious leaders consistently hand-picked scriptures of hell fire and brimstone or dogmatic regulations when they needed to assert a little more control over their listeners. Once control was regained, then came some joyful promise of the hereafter if all requirements were strictly adhered to. Yes, each scripture recited was indeed in the Bible but the messages seemed true according to whatever personal message the speaker wanted to impart to his parishioners...all based on his own self-appointed interpretation of them. I assert to you today that I too am currently choosing to live by my own God-given interpretations which spill over with God's infinite love for us and that overflow with scriptures containing our inheritance as God's heirs and heiresses. These scriptures are used as guides for my life among many writings instead of being used as isolated interpretations that are designed to bind, scare, and confuse in order to gain some human oriented result! I strongly urge you to do the same. By doing this, you assume responsibility for your peace, your light, your prosperity, your actions, your outcomes, and ultimately your relationship with your Source and Creator. You determine that your response to an action by anyone outside of you is 100% within your control and that your reactions will be lovingly performed in a manner that is befitting your God-plan, causing your situation to become exactly what you make of it. Do I believe in the Bible? Yes, but not over God's timely relevant voice within me. Yes, this is new thought for you as it was for me. But the interpretation of others is far too risky in that their inner guidance might have given them a certain interpretation for themselves and NOT others. And let's face it, individual interpretations change from person to person and over time. In fact, from one person to the next, interpretations never remain the same...AND I AM SO HAPPY ABOUT THAT! I am free to hear God tell me what He wants me to know as an individual daughter and temple of His with an individual plan for my life that is unique to me. The Bible has changed from language to language, from version to version and from century to century but God's infinite love for me remains the same. The freedom in this is that I...You become a co-creator of your life because you are made in the image of THE CREATOR. You do what the Creator does no matter what it is (also known as being like Christ). What does The Creator do? He creates...and so shall you. He loves, and so shall you. He is light, and so shall you be. He is peace, and since He is inside of you, you shall have and be peace. He is The Giver...and so shall you be. He is The Savior, and since you are His image, you shall be what others need to see in order for them to be like Him and they shall be saved from outside influences and will be guided from within. If you seek to absolve yourself of this active and reactive responsibility, then you reinforce an inner lazy false belief that "poor you" cannot help your situation because others won't do their part to help you. This is the case in many of our situations of lack, frustration, anger, poverty, addiction, hate, marital discord, etc. It is the lazy way out...except you don't escape the situation, you maintain the manifestation of it.

Why Did God Allow Preachers, Gurus, Popes, and Religious Leaders To Be Here?

So why then were Pastors, Teachers, Apostles, Prophets appointed...(Ephesians 4:11)? Ephesians 4:13 answers this question by saying that they should help to perfect, to work, and to edify, "Till we all come in the unity (Oneness) of the faith, and of the knowledge of the Son of God, unto a perfect man...". It is clear that the goal of appointing these positions was to unify ALL in perfect love. That is the goal that each one of us should have and this is indeed the goal of this writer. It is to be the living embodiment of the phrase, "WE ARE ONE". This scripture then brings up the question, "Are the Pastors, Teachers, Apostles, etc. promoting INCLUSION, UNITY and LOVE? After years and years of attending church services, meetings, and spiritual gatherings, ask yourself that question. Have you been included, unified, and loved? Have YOU been promoting inclusion, unity and love or have you been a parasitic spectator? It is very clear by the many, many factions, denominations, splinter groups, spinoffs, and defectors in conjunction with public coups and private mutinies within the church, religious groups, and new thought groups and cliques that in fact disunity is being encouraged and enacted from the top down. "Don't go to this church or that one because they don't believe in this or that. They sin this way and not the way we do so they are not right. Don't fellowship with these people because they have a gay choir director, don't hang out with these because they are not the same kind of Christians that we are, let's just stick to the good ole way!" Well, these directives usually came from the top down and were completely counter to THE LIFE of JESUS whom you say you know. Who did Jesus surround himself with? I'll wait...so much emphasis is placed on isolated scriptures that many have chosen to (mis)interpret the very Spirit and life of Jesus and not only do you negate his life but many teach against being like him. And so, those wolves are dismissed as the time has come for unity, edification and love to take over. All outside of love will be replaced, like it or not.

So, who then, if these appointees have failed miserably, should take their places...because they will be replaced as part of the inevitable imminent growth and evolutionary process that we are smack in the middle of RIGHT NOW? Well, let us first understand why we the people elected to follow them? We chose to follow some of these "appointees" because many of us believed that God had given them a special message for us that we should get in line if we wanted to please God and make it to heaven or at the scariest, stay out of hell. We were told this and followed out of ignorance, or out of "sheep hood (just follow because we said so)" and for many, they followed because of a genuine desire to please the God of their understanding and perhaps reap a heavenly reward — never mind any earthly rewards. Aside from the micro reasons for our blind faith, it is the belief of this writer that in the big picture of growth and evolution to higher consciousness, we were allowed by the Creator to take this path because at the time this bible verse was written and up until recently, the faith and awareness of the masses needed to be gently raised to an introductory level lesson of the ideas of God in order to impart a basic faith prior to the "meat" of the Word. This could only be accomplished first by exposing us to God as the most powerful outside force working for us from heaven and if we called and begged and acted with sincerity He might come down if He saw fit and give us a small boost of whatever we needed to make it through to the next church meeting. Great truths of God are often shrouded in bias, misunderstanding or outright lies when delivered by man and the truth of Gods infinite power is no exception.

This exposure to God's omnipotence, like many exposures (good or bad), came with an overflow of propaganda, fear mongering, predatory scare tactics, and resulting casualties in the form of those who have given up before ever knowing the unconditional Love of God our Source. Many have decided not to believe in Him at all ever again because the message of God's infinite, unconditional, all-encompassing love was hidden behind an avalanche of greed, judgment, exclusion, hatred, and most of all, fear when in fact God's love is infinitely for everyone and cannot be earned. And so with this new revelation of a truly infinite God, many are opening again to the knowledge of God as He truly is...a living Love who dwells inside of them just as He dwells in those who have come to know and live their purpose. Not to be misconstrued, some preachers and gurus did learn to listen to the God in them early on, thus their influence over many and by this, they persuaded the masses who in turn contributed greatly to the lives of abundance and freedom that most of these leaders have been fortunate enough to live. But the time of the religious leader who "gets rich quick"has passed...the masses must now awaken to their own true purpose and inner God which will open the door to the abundance and love that they are awakening to find inside of themselves. This means that they are no longer absolved of the love and responsibility of living their destiny. All are lovingly held accountable for the use and multiplication of their gifts and talents and they must hear from THE GOD in them for themselves regarding their purpose in life. When they hear the unmistakable experience of God, they will know it without a doubt for He speaks through our love and passion for life. He gives us a love and passion for something and tells us to create a life around what we love to do and He will multiply it. We are held accountable for our happiness, our passion for life by living it. If we do not live it, the price we pay is unhappiness, lack, unfulfilled loneliness, stress, and slavery followed by our funerals...God doesn't want this for us! However, this accountability is not distributed by anyone outside of the God-Self. A preacher, prophet, rabbi, Imam or other religious person can only deliver to you their interpretation of the written words of great books such as the Bible, Quran or Torah which can be helpful but should not be the final word for our lives-the final word comes from within. THE DIVINE INTERPRETATION MEANT FOR EACH ONE OF US INDIVIDUALLY (SOME CALL IT A RHEMA WORD) CAN ONLY COME FROM THE GOD WITHIN EACH OF US INDIVIDUALLY AND WILL BE SOLELY FOR US as we seek it. This Rhema word is often mistaken as given to all when it is really being given to the one speaking it for their own personal lives. However, your specific feelings and desires were given to you for the precise purpose of prompting you in the direction of your choosing which automatically releases The Creative Force (God) to honor those feelings and desires and conspire on your behalf for 100% success NO MATTER WHAT! If you are frustrated and unfulfilled, that is your memo and the reason to look to your inner Source to show you and to make manifest all that you already are. And unlike hellfire and brimstone messages (fear based), God delivers His message for your life with love. The promptings, feelings and desires of your heart are "messages" given so that you may do what you love and become your highest self.

Coming from what I consider the best scenario of a religious background along with my growth environment and outside influences, I always felt within me that I needed to do certain things and perform certain rituals (say certain prayers, use certain oils, etc.) in order to feel like God might take kindly or pitifully on me and reward me with an occasional blessing. This worked on a few occasions because of my mental attachment to them. What I grew to understand about these oils, actions, and other assistive devices (I call them "spiritual prosthetics" which are substitutes by definition) is that they were psychologically enslaving me into believing that if something wasn't done using that particular item, then my action was not acceptable to God, not to mention me being acceptable without any props! And woe be unto me if I didn't parrot the terms and phrases the way everyone around me did…WHOA! Then it was automatically the devil and I was "dabbling in witchcraft". This still happens on social media today as well. If I don't call my Creator what others do, then it never fails that someone will "correct" me-my post won't be "liked" by some "church" folks and that is okay. And guess what? God has not gotten angry with me not once over what I call Him because He knows that deep within the recesses of my Soul, even the current words that I use to describe Him are gravely inadequate at best. He is indeed indescribable, so what I call Him is best reflected when He sees my Soul. My Soul is a reflection of Him! He knows how I feel about Him by the life I live and He keeps blessing me just to prove He is pleased with me! I'm free from within! I now know that I am ENOUGH and worthy of abundance, an amazing life and a free conscience! I no longer feel that I need to earn each blessing, or earn that period of rest, or work my way into the space of feeling loved. I can feel freedom and love all day every day! Fortunately and ironically, I had to be freed from the opinions of others in order to experience this true freedom in life that has come to me.

Prior to my God-experience, life's bondage made it difficult to feel loved by God since I had no idea HOW to earn those things. In error, I guessed I would do without them. I then tried to fill that hole with outside substances and actions. It wasn't until my own personal, intimate experience with God ALONE that I knew that there was a far better plan for me. It has been said that if you do what you love, you will never work another day in your life...This is how we were designed to live-this is the plan with love as its base. God loves us so much that He wants us to do what we love to do with our lives for the rest of our lives. Many of the wealthy know this and become wealthy by following what they may describe as their gut instincts, intuition, "that voice", however, upon talking with them, they say it is the voice of God (The God in them). Our lives were given to us to be fulfilled, intelligent, happy, prosperous, abundant, filled with love, completely void of condemnation, absent of shame, and free from guilt and filled with purpose and dominion. As more and more people come to the realization that the true and living God is on the inside of them, today's mosques, synagogues, and churches may find fewer and fewer occupants lest they shift to become sharers of the Light which always points others to the inner God and no one else regardless of any boundaries, divisions or classifications...also known as separators of humankind. These separators are the antithesis of God for we are One with Him and cannot be separated from Him, thus we cannot be separated from one another. He is always with us and we with Him.

When it was written in Hebrews 13:5 and Deuteronomy 31:6 that, "I will never leave you nor forsake you", what do you think this meant? And if The Source of All Creation is always with you, where do you perceive His location to be in relationship to you...on your shoulder?...perhaps on your back?....or maybe in front of you?...All of those are correct since He is everywhere but He resides inside of you...in what

He calls our temple. Our earthly bodily temples house our souls and our consciousness which is made for the Source to live in and breathe in and have His being. Genesis 2:7 says that The Source of All Creation "breathed into his (man's) nostrils the breath of life and man became a living being". This meant ALL humankind with no exclusions. If God did not exclude anyone, then who are we to exclude anyone. Is not God's breath inside of you giving you life? He is inside of you guiding you if you will but acknowledge His presence there. Your acknowledgement of His presence inside of you will consistently remind you of who you really are. The only mediator between you and God, between you and all there is...is inside of you. Jesus as well as Buddha, Ghandi, Mohammed, and many others were mediators who pointed us to God dwelling within us thereby eliminating any need for earthly barriers, divisions, walls, blockages, veils, or people to stand between God and His creation-you and me.

Your acknowledgement of Him inside of you is your acceptance of Him...and your acceptance of yourself as Him and He as you. Your acceptance of Him inside of you is your acceptance of the fact that you are not broken, so you need no one and no earthly thing to fix you. You are a perfectly imperfect, whole, complete, loving, safe, powerful, being formed from energy that is pure love. This knowledge is the unstoppable effect of higher consciousness.

Are You Afraid?

Why do you fret, worry, and run around ashamed and some even gloat when church scandal unfolds...when some preachers, ministers, rabbis, and others of the diocese prove their humanness? Why does your faith fail you and then you become disillusioned, bitter, and hopeless? Did you not know that there is no one on the planet that should be held to a higher standard than the God in you? It is because you do not know who the God in you is, that you would now still look to anyone else for God's purpose, message, example and blessing for your life. The word "preacher" is defined as "one who proclaims, instructs or makes known by sermon. A "guru" is defined as "a master teacher or instructor". For so long, our pedestal to God has been occupied by someone other than God because of their defined title. This is our own doing and it is now time for us to acknowledge and accept the result of our decisions. We have chosen to let every other human being hold this sacred spot and then we become bitter and sometimes destructive when their humanness disappoints us. Our view of God and ourselves has too long hinged on the behavior of others, rather than of ourselves. When humans falter, (and we all do at some point) some even hold God accountable and move away from Him because of what others do which is simply confirm their humanness. Church scandals illustrate this fact. The complications of church scandals have made us tell ourselves that the life event is so big and embarrassing that we could never go through that kind of public humiliation and that the magnitude of the shame is only reserved for those on the level of preacher, pastor, cardinal, head rabbi, imam, leader, etc. Oh, but we are underestimating our Source who has taken many of us through situations much greater on a personal level in our own lives, situations that tested the very core of our beings and brought us through it. It is time for each of us to assume full responsibility for our own journey. So do not be distracted and wax weak and critical when yet another religious leader moves below public or private expectation because this movement is a part of each of our journeys...and it is not the fault or responsibility of the one who did not meet your expectation to justify or validate your God. You are to continue to love equally the one who has proven their humanness, and still journey with them into higher consciousness. You see, when you become disheartened it is your own thinking that causes you to be so, so change your thoughts and you will no longer be disheartened but strengthened knowing that God has not gone anywhere, He is still inside of you and in control of every situation. So long as God is inside of you, you need not look to any other human for authentication.

Yet another outcome of a so called scandal is our reaction to it. A life event (scandal) happens and we act out and behave badly in answer to it. Then we go to others, in most cases right back to these same religious institutions to seek to feel forgiven for our actions, to repurchase yet another golden ticket into heaven or to become realigned with our indwelling Source.

The discomfort that accompanies our behavior happens in the institutionalized thoughts (cognitive dissonance) of those who then seek this feeling of forgiveness. The vulnerability of seeking is what has been preyed upon by some in organized religion even to this day. Over time, the media, the government and many in society have used this scenario of the poor person who sought relief from "sin" but was instead victimized and robbed to accuse the religious of predatory behavior. While there is some truth to that claim in many cases, the parishioner is not so unknowing as many are led to believe. Many religious leaders have been blamed for "scamming the blind and unlearned parishioners" out of their livelihoods. But, to the contrary, parishioners consistently prove that their level of understanding of their actions and the actions of their leadership is remarkable. If one can stand in competent assessment of their fallen leaders, then they have that same ability to suitably sum up their own actions. But instead of going directly to the God within, many people have been taught to go and "make amends" in some public fashion to earn God's approval. This has been repeated in many people's lives from birth to death. Many found ease of conscience through rites, rituals and payments to gurus, preachers and the church that, while their lives were no better, their minds were eased at the thought of a God who could be satiated through some human act. They were convinced that this ritual would make God feel better about them if their act was filtered through a "cleaner vessel more close to God" then themselves for they were distanced by their actions, not knowing that the perception of a cleaner vessel is strictly a state of mind and nothing more for we are all equally worthy.

This ability to think and self-assess is making way for raised material outcomes and spiritual awareness among mankind. As the consciousness of mankind is being raised, the level of responsibility for our journeys to knowing God can no longer be blamed on ANY human leader. To do so places that person in the space that should rightfully be occupied by the God in us. Bishop T.D. Jakes insists that, "If you deify me, you eliminate you", meaning if you put him (the preacher, leader, guru, etc.) in the place of or in between YOUR SOURCE, it makes the preacher philosophically closer to God than you and you can no longer go straight to God ~ you become of lesser value by your own comparison and by your own word and belief. We now know for ourselves who God really is and that we are acceptable to Him regardless of outside circumstances, situations, and human conditions. We know that He hears us directly, intimately, lovingly without the judgments, interference, or interpretation of any man. We are required now to release our need to place mental/spiritual distance between ourselves and God via other human beings. We have willingly digested a huge misperception at best unless we come to know that we could not be any closer to God then He in us and we in Him which is the permanent state of our lives. That will never change regardless of our actions. With no one to blame but the state of our own thoughts for the perceived distance from God, the middleman to God is now removed from our perception and processes (the veil is rent in two) and we are to open our minds and hearts to God for ourselves. This message will be called blasphemous by many in the church who stand to lose much should they be removed from the position of broker, liaison or middleman to God but anger and fear won't make this message any less relevant and eye opening. Yes, we should not fail to assemble ourselves together but to assemble means come together in our higher consciousness and if a literal meaning is needed (which it is not), we should gather to edify one another and help each person learn the voice of God for himself...no pedestal needed but all are equal in the process. Yes, we are the leadership that we have been waiting for.

The Great Coming Together

So no more dry, uninspired, ritualistic meetings that serve to do nothing more than satisfy a Sunday morning obligation. There is a new purpose for our gatherings. The purpose of our spiritual gatherings and meetings is now to come together and to share AMONG each other growth experiences, spiritual revelations and higher self-truths that will help to edify one another and share Light, rather than to elevate, and promote any one person above all others as "God's one messenger" for we are all the voice of God. In these group gatherings, coordinators can facilitate open dialogue from the hearts and minds of all as we expand and grow together into higher consciousness. Those who listen for Gods indwelling voice more deeply must admonish others to do the same but no formal title of "holiness" is necessary to help others to the Light. Having come to this revelation, what then is to become of many of the large congregations, the megachurches, and many of those flashy charismatic preachers who have helped to lead us into the current state of affairs? Ironically, there is no gloom and doom report, but there is a note that their positions will cease to exist as we know them today for reasons varying from huge public scandals to the changing tide in the spiritual atmosphere and for many parishioners, the sheer boredom of it all. People need more, have evolved and thirst for applicable, higher substance. Today's leadership will have to become one of many with seekers and re-member who they are so that they can use their God-given skills to do as any other enlightened individual would do-point others to the Light...minus the pedestal. This new paradigm will not be allowed to model the old "highly untouchable priest, lowly sin-laden sheep" archetype. In I Corinthians 2:12 this model is nullified, "...*the Spirit who is from God, so that we may know the things **freely** given to* *us by God"*. This is to say that since God does give freely The Spirit then it is for all to have, not just a few. The sheep now know that they are equally as acceptable, lovable and loved unconditionally by God and need no broker or middleman. They can have a direct and intimate relationship with God for themselves...one that this author has come to know. And now it is the purpose of all who are awakened to point others to that wonderful Light...within. For who knows each individual better than the God in each of us? This way, our success can only be attributed to God and our relationship with Him just as our failures can only be attributed to God's love for us through growth opportunities. We all have the tools and abilities to rise to higher knowing through these opportunities. We have no one to credit but The Source Of All Creation within us! How exciting and sure! This is great news for most of us, but unsettling to some. Why? Because this new thought is not something that can be capitalized on using the old models of church and organizational growth. There is no one organization who holds the power or key to this way of life. This is a very exciting and new concept for those who are waking up but is against the purpose and teaching of organized religion because it strips them of their lucrative hold on people who can now go to God for themselves. Proverbs 3:5-6 says, "Trust in the LORD with all thine heart; and lean not unto thine own understanding. In all thy ways acknowledge him, and he shall direct thy paths." People now realize that their strength to move into purpose comes from the God within them rather than someone or something outside of themselves. If the strength, abundance and purpose came from something outside of us, we would have already figured it out and used it to our benefit after decades and decades of listening to others who followed the God in them as it led them into leadership and abundance. There is no one "leader of the people" but God. Why? Because this new thought is a way whereby each person seeks to know their own personal inner God for themselves. There are no hard and fast rituals about anything outside of ourselves; no particular uniform to wear, no particular person to lead the way (for we all are priests once awakened), no act that excludes anyone willing to awaken, no status that is excluded, no specific building to go to on any specific day of the week (only as you will it to be so), no one type of music to listen to, no human action or ritual to perform, nothing of any kind except a wanting to "re-member" or "re-cognize" the voice and love of God. The new leadership is all of us collectively working together and moving forward as we listen to the God inside of us leading us to higher consciousness as we lead others to God's Light and Love. That is what a great servant will help each newcomer to do, to re-cognize (put into the thoughts again that which indicates that the thought was in the mind previously but forgotten) and to re-member (to assemble again in the mind). This movement is everything together...everyone together...come as you are and be fully accepted NONJUDGMENTALLY...bring your talents, skills and abilities so that they can be multiplied into the highest form of YOU. And everything must be done in love and freedom regardless of race, creed, color, sexual orientation, social status, background, or life choices. This rare, new openness and nonjudgmental acceptance will be difficult for the human race as a whole at first but this writer is convinced that it WILL happen starting with each person reading this and waking up. This is a movement that can be duplicated in every neighborhood, every language, every socioeconomic echelon, and on every continent. But how is that possible with so many different versions of the movement? It is easy. Each and every one of us will experience that same "inner knowing" that can only come from the Source Of All Creation. Signs of this inner knowing are the same in each of us regardless of any outside factors that would have us believe that we are "different". For example, if I travel to another country and meet someone with non-formal education which differs from my own formal learning but they have been taught to recognize the God in themselves, we will, upon making eye contact and/or meeting each other in passing, already feel a kindred spirit between us that lets us know that we have "met our spiritual match" and can move on confidently knowing that we have just seen God...again. This voids the notion of the necessity of any one specially deified human to "chase a thousand (negative thoughts) or put ten thousand to flight" in our stead but confirms that we can join two or three together (in thought, in prayer, by phone or internet or in person, in Spirit, etc.) and accomplish the same mission and have God in the midst. It is an underlying fact that this new thought movement cannot be organized in terms of an institutional body such as the Catholic Church or any other religious group. Many a self-proclaimed "guru" is finding this out the hard way. This new thought movement is, quite paradoxically, an individual yet collective process that gains momentum via critical mass. Since the God that reigned inside of Jesus is the same God that reigns in each of us, it only serves to bear witness that each of us is either seeking to awaken or is already awakening to our true inner God-ness at this moment in time by divine providence. While none of us feels the need to join any group, sect, church or organization (this is a main marker of those who are waking up-to find God for themselves), it is okay to feel that nudge to come together with others who are experiencing similar signs of waking up as we have felt. The great and running theme of this way of life is that each and every thought, feeling, and past action is not only acceptable but is open for discussion since there is nothing new under the sun and none of us are the first to have such thoughts...freedom to love is the only way this new thought life will work. Shall we give it a try? I say yes...what say you?

Becoming Unstoppable: No More Waiting

"Well, I'm new to this so I need to sit down, be quiet and learn"....NOT SO! You can begin to share with others upon learning even one new thought, idea, or way. Open sharing with others as they invite you to share dialogue breaks down walls of uneasiness and procrastination and sets the process in motion right away but in real time. No need for pushy dogmatic rhetoric, just peaceful, joyful, love in its fullness. So then how can someone who has only recognized the God in them for a short period of time be able to give a word as powerful and helpful as someone who has been a preacher or guru for many years? Because all humans can truly hear and receive the basic message of love that can and should be delivered to as many as possible daily. It is not because of religious or spiritual age but because of their openness to share the love of God. It does not take God years and years to speak profound relevance as was believed in times past. LOVE CAN BE PASSED ON THROUGH ACTION IMMEDIATELY, DAILY. I remember hearing so often that only those with many years in church and the blessing of the "presiding elders" could go before the people and speak because only they had a word that God gave them that those younger "in the Lord" could not hear...Isn't that placing severe limits on God's ability to speak to each of us? We are all guilty of placing our own earthen limits on the Creator of All Things and then we wonder why we cannot seem to reach the next level in our lives. We can see ourselves no higher than poverty because our view of God's true creative ability in ourselves has been minimized down to what we are capable of without acknowledgement of His greatness inside of us. If our success depends on seeing the accomplishments of those around us, or what the television and society feeds us, rather than what the One who created everything has done, then we are impoverished by our own thoughts. As a man thinketh in his heart, so is he (Proverbs 23:7). Society through the media works especially hard to reinforce the falsehood that you don't have what you need to be successful when all you need is to follow the prompting of the indwelling Spirit and the Spirit will conspire on your behalf to make all things align for your success. You have all the tools you need to manifest your desires but if you don't know this, you will continue to purchase pseudo-manifestations which will keep you in poverty and poverty then becomes a never ending circle. No one knows more about what you need than the God in you. Yes, others are used to help you remember what the God in you already knows but none are closer to God than another...than you. As for the notion that only those who are "mature in the Lord" can hear from him, well we only need to look at the overwhelming number of "fallen preachers" who were born, bred and trained in church but who have seemingly lost everything as a result...of turning out to be human. We created these great catastrophes because we as parishioners, followers, seekers, and congregants had placed a person between us and God in error. If He is in us, what sense does it make to allow someone outside of us to rule our spiritual lives? For who can rule better than God? You might respond to this question by saying that some people need guidance because they just can't manage themselves. While this is true, ultimately the only guidance that should be given them is to teach them to listen to the voice of God inside of them who will guide them into all truth. Well, you might say, I don't know what God sounds like! The moment you begin to wonder what His voice sounds like, your journey begins. When I was a little girl, I remember hearing the voice of God on so many occasions...each time it was for my safety, growth, and learning. I didn't know at that time that it was the God in me guiding me but now that I have re-learned His voice, I know that He never left me but was always there. His voice was loud as a child until I was taught to listen to every adult on the planet instead of Him. His voice then became just a whisper, always accompanied by a feeling, an instinct that consistently prompted an emotion and an action. As I came into recognition of my journey, that voice inside of me prompted me to quiet all other voices for 5 months in preparation for my purpose …no television, no internet in the home, no cellular phone, no preachers, no church, no one…but the Source of All Creation. It was in that time that I relearned, remembered, God's voice. It became much more prominent and I grew to trust it. I have since come to love it, to cherish it, to follow it, to trust it, to live by it and it is the only voice I know without a doubt.

Where Does Prosperity Come Into The Picture?

Yet another result of putting another person in between you and your Source is that this person will need something from you for their services. They will need something for their time, their effort, their privileged status, their special place as broker to the Source...and rightfully so. Our direct line to the Source is a conduit for prosperity, energy and inspiration to go back and forth. Money is energy. Therefore, this broker is correct in asking that you support his place as conduit or broker to your direct Source. You must pay the person that you have placed in the pathway of your Source because as the Laws of God dictate, the blessings still continue on their path to you...whoever is in the pathway of you and your Source will be blessed by default. And know that their blessing will be a portion of yours that, had they not been hired as broker, would come to you. You can continue to keep that person in your line of blessing, or you can choose to receive directly from your Source. Either way you are blessed, but in differing measures. Many have grown sour, in error, because they chose to place someone else in their line of contact with God and then became envious that the person lived better than they did...not understanding that the jealousy and envy is out of place since the choice to put another human being in that direct line to God was of their own free will. Some might see this as "spiritual anarchy" but it is not. It is giving full acknowledgement to the God in you which He and you fully deserve. This is what is needed in order for you to realize your full self...your full worth...your full expansion into your purpose, the REAL, FULL, TRUE, ENDLESS POWER of God without the limitations of our thinking as if He were a man. Putting another in your line of contact to God is tantamount to you paying someone else for you to use your own brain to think. You are now detached from your sense of power to change your circumstances into full abundance. This leaves you feeling as though you "still need to become" instead of knowing that you already are what you should be to live and work in your purpose. We have been brainwashed into thinking that many religious leaders are already in the place that they need to be to work in their purpose BUT WE ARE NOT. He/She is fixed but we are broken. The result of this self-induced brainwashing is our current condition which includes our continuing to subscribe, to buy, to seek, to petition other humans for permission to live in our fullness. As we awaken to our rightful identities, we will begin immediately working in our perfect purpose today. But we are constantly told that there is something ELSE that we need to do, learn, acquire, buy, WAIT FOR or pray for before we are ready to move into the lives we so desperately want. And many religious leaders have (knowingly or

73

unknowingly) made sure that we feel this man-imposed or self-imposed false deficit. The result of this fallacy is one that I mentioned in the "Edict of Humanity" section of my book, "5 Ways To Take Your Peace To Work With You" (AMAZON.com). Many people live in pain and die in misery because WE have not risen to the promise of our calling to help them. And most frustrating for you is that you live in misery because you have not acknowledged your authority to go directly to God for instructions on living in your highest, most abundant purpose beginning right this moment. Is this suggesting that we don't need each other? No. We need each other now more than ever. Do we need preachers, gurus, and religious leaders at all? We need them BUT not as one who stands between God and man, not as one who must be on a pedestal above the masses but as equals in the very same capacity as we need each other. We need each other as equals who can help one another on our paths to rise to higher consciousness as never before...not a fleshly deity who we have assigned the position of a human form of our God, for we are all forms of God in the flesh (heirs and joint heirs {Romans 8:17}, sons and daughters {2 Corinthians 6:18}, created in His image {Genesis 9:6}). We are assembling together in mind, body and spirit to be our best without an idol to represent the God that we see in ourselves. If we need a physical representation of God, we should seek the closest mirror for we are made in His image and likeness.

All of us are blessed with the desire to do things, to accomplish things, but there is a disconnection between the desire and the knowing that we can do it enough to get up and make it happen. There is a gap between our desire and our will to do it...this gap is filled when we understand that there is nothing that the Creator of All Things who resides inside of us cannot do. His voice, his promptings will always lead us to the next steps to take in the process of becoming our full true highest selves. We just need to learn His voice and listen to it without fail. There have been many times that we have been prompted by the indwelling Spirit to do something, but we stopped because we chose to listen to a "professional" be it preacher, manager, scientist, or doctor, who admonished us otherwise. In most instances, we simply caved in to the spoken and unspoken pressure from society at large. Later, we were shown why we should have listened to our "first mind", our intuition, the voice of creativity and success, the Spirit. Now more than ever we are being shown that just because someone has a title and years of higher learning, they still may not be qualified on a spiritual level to speak into each individual life as if they are the Source of All Creation (God) - Wall Street's best and brightest with the cleanest backgrounds proved that we are better off listening to the true Source of our abundance

FIRST before placing our faith in earthly credentials! That is the beauty of God. He dwells in, speaks to and speaks through even those of us with extensive, taboo and controversial pasts (and even more so because of what we have been through). What love!! None of us are beyond the love of our Creator. NOTHING can separate us from this love! But as I have admonished others, do not take my word or anyone's word for it. DON'T BELIEVE ANYTHING I SAY, nor any preacher, guru, counselor, religious figurehead or others but experience it for yourself... Don't just read about it, don't just hear about it, and don't just believe it simply because everyone around you believed it...open to the experience of God in You. This is the only way that you will know what is true. What have you got to lose?

If you were designed to think exactly like everyone else, you would be just like everyone else...what higher calling is there in that? You might think yourself weird or different because everyone else says you are but keep going in the direction that you are being led...then you will understand why you have felt so different all of this time and so will everyone else, just as they did with all great leaders of the past and present. It is by Divine Design. But here is the best part about God's Divine Design-have you ever heard of two people on opposite sides of the world inventing the very same product at the same time (such as has happened with the invention of the airplane) without ever meeting or talking to each other? Well, the very same thing is happening with you and your "weird" new awakening, except that many who have already experienced it recognize it. It is known as the, "Collective Consciousness".

How Do I Begin My Journey To Waking Up?

How will I know that I am awake? You will know because you will feel awake, you will know who you are and what your purpose in life is at any given time. But most of all, you will not look outside for yourself for love, peace, abundance, creativity, or happiness. You won't have to switch churches, groups or cliques ever again because you will start being the person that you are looking for every time you leave a church or group and go join another one just because someone in the one you left disappointed you by showing you their human glory with all of it's perfect imperfections. You will know without doubt that you are connected directly to the Source of All Creation. And how do you get to this point? Take these steps as often as possible throughout the day and throughout the week until they become a beautiful life practice:

1) You must first quiet all outside noise-go away from all interference. Move into a place of solitude for however long it takes for you to be able to quiet you thoughts. For some people this is a few minutes in their bedroom with a "Do Not Disturb" sign on the door. For others, this is an empty office on a quiet end of the building. And for others still, it can range from a weeklong retreat to a month long sabbatical to a year or more of the same. The purpose of the solitude is so that you can connect or reconnect with God directly, without any outside intrusion. It is important that all outside voices, opinions, judgments, and admonitions be silenced so that the voice of God can be clear and recognizable within you. Do not worry about whether or not He might want to talk to you for He promised

that if you seek His voice, you will find Him, He will answer. You are to enter into this space with nothing but love and gratitude.

2) Next, breathe deeply as you focus on quieting all thoughts. When I first began this process, I would focus on one affirmative thought of gratitude only and repeat it both aloud and inwardly. This one thought seemed to calm and quiet all others. It was a thought of complete, isolated gratitude. I simply thought the words, "Thank you...Thank you...Thank you". I did this repeatedly until I began to feel it deep within me. As gratitude enveloped me and I became gratitude, I wept with peaceful thankfulness as appreciation penetrated my entire body to the core of my soul. Your experience may be different and that is ok too. At first, you may only

be able to silence all thoughts outside of gratitude for just a short period of time but with practice this meditation of gratitude, will expand and lengthen. Gratitude is the attractor of blessings, abundance, clarity and all things good and perfect.

3) Once you have silenced the negativity and opened up to gratitude, you may then want to listen to meditational music or spoken word affirmations (Youtube is filled with these wonderful recordings that affirm only abundance, peace, love, prosperity and anything else that you might want to manifest). Do this until you feel and believe what you have heard and meditated on. Do this every day so that your positive reprogramming is consistently reinforced. I prefer to do this right before going

to bed and immediately upon waking in the morning.

4) VERY IMPORTANT! Begin to invite your purpose into your life. If you do not know what your purpose in life is, then ask The Creator to show you. Chances are, He will simply ask you, "what do you love to do?" or "what are you passionate about?". You were given your passions and feelings to guide you into your purpose. You wouldn't feel love and passion for something if it were not meant for you. God created all of the things we love so that we can enjoy them, period. Once you recognize what you have passion for, then begin to work towards making the life that you want. Begin to fill your life with it as often as possible, not only to become a master at it but to reinforce the love that you

have for it so that your passion can be fed and grow. It has been said over the centuries many times and in many ways that if you do what you love, you will never work another day in your life...and take it from me, THIS IS ONE OF THE HIGHEST TRUTHS EVER! Your goal is to create a life that no longer requires an annual vacation away from it. You are to love the precious life that you have been given.

5) Next, create a vision board. Your vision will become living energy for you as you construct it! Put EVERYTHING that you want in life on it, leaving nothing out. If you want a certain type of home, find illustrations that closely reflect what you want and put them on your vision board. If you want a certain amount of abundance, find or create an illustration of it and put it on your

vision board. Do not be ashamed or shy about what you want but be bold and clear about your vision and what you will to manifest in your life. Once constructed, study it daily without fail. Close your eyes and visualize what it will feel like when your vision actually happens and you are driving up to your dream home, parking your car, and putting the key in the door. As you open the door, visualize who will be there if anyone. How will it smell? Will it be warm and inviting on a cold fall day or will it be crisp and cool inside as you escape a 92 degree heat index outside? Continuously picture in your mind that you have already obtained that which you seek. This type of visualization should be done often throughout the day as your enthusiasm and motivation are reinforced. When your thoughts are reprogrammed, renewed, and transformed, your vision will have one course to take and that course is manifestation, plain and simple.

6) Once your purpose becomes clear to you and you are armed with a positive thought life along with both a spiritual life that is a reflection of God in you, and a clear vision, then begin to work your purpose. Make at least one move daily or even hourly in the direction of the manifestation of your purpose. Take one step daily towards your fullest potential, your highest self, all the while knowing that God wants for you what you want for you. Repeat these steps as often as possible and watch how your life becomes exactly what you envisioned because you have gone straight to God for yourself and taken active steps toward being the person you

want to be! As you move in your purpose as God has shown it to you (God asks, "What do you love to do?), you will begin to notice that the God in you will continue to show you who you really are. Your highest vision of who you are is exactly who God would have you be.

As you continue to awaken to your path, and grow and expand in all areas of your life, joyfully acknowledge each victory, large or small, that occurs as a result of your decision to wake up and live! And there will be many. There are some wonderful practices that will help you on your path to knowing yourself in the image of God:

1. In order to make positive thoughts a reflex instead of automatically generating and accepting the seemingly negative thoughts that come so quickly and easily to us, begin

to observe your thoughts and how they make you feel so that you can recognize the negative programming and begin to erase the thoughts that have plagued you all of your life. Then you can begin to refill your thoughts, your mind, your ears, your heart and your mouth with positivity that will manifest the good in your life that is meant to be.

2. Guard what you watch! Just say no to all things negative including news shows, reality T.V. shows, negative and violent movies, etc. That leaves very little else to watch which means your time will not be consumed with hours upon hours of watching television, for what goes in will come out. Your life can only manifest what is inside of you, your

thoughts. This negative media is designed to create and feed fear in various forms. During your life change, you will need the space that these negativities use for more positive, productive, helpful purposes that lead to higher consciousness. The quickest way to be rid of negative thoughts is first to stop the onslaught of negativity before it becomes a thought (turn off the TV!) and then begin to purposefully reprogram what enters the gates of your consciousness so that it reflects and manifests goodness and abundance through the consumption of all things positive. No, you are not putting your head in the sand and pretending not to see negativity around you, but you are acknowledging that the negativity will not be

an active participant in your life.

3. Guard what you hear! No negative music!

    Steer clear of negative, idle talk that does

    not offer solutions to issues or events.

4. Guard who you surround yourself with! Try

    to spend more time with like-minded people

    and those wanting to open to their purpose.

    For while we are to include all people in our

    lives, we should offer ourselves a steady

    stream of positive energy in order to better

    connect with those who are not yet awake

    or not as far along on their path as we are.

    We will connect with all people as we move

    about our lives and should seek the good in

    everyone while guarding the gates of our

    minds, hearts and spirits. Speak, share, and

commune with positive spirits often for you and they will exchange valuable insights on your path that will assist in manifesting the life that you envision for yourself. For those people who may be challenges in your life, you may not spend time with them as much but you are to love them and ask The Creator to help you to see them in a more uplifting way that will lead you to think and speak positive, uplifting and abundant affirmations about them, yourself, and your purpose. Know that they are okay just as they are for they too are images of God. This is especially important whenever fear tries to enter your thoughts or actions to cause you to respond negatively to them. In time, love will live through you and you will be able to love and accept them as they are without trying to change or "fix" them for they are not broken.

What Now?

Having said all that is written here, since the God in you is now "in charge", what is to become of the thousands of churchgoers who depend on someone outside of themselves for their motivation and purpose? To this I say, "SOMETHING WONDERFUL IS HAPPENING RIGHT NOW!" The people who have awakened are and will continue to re-create their awakening in others and this will be the way that the great awakening will continue to spread around the globe. Does awakening mean that you will no longer want to go to church? Can you be awake and still love church, singing, fellowshipping, and giving? The answer to these questions is this: If those activities are a part of your purpose and are pathways to further growth, expansion and enlightenment, then you will freely do them as you wish, however, you will not feel obligated, duty-bound, or bored by them. Enlightenment is your permission to do what you love to do and know that God is with you always while you do it! Awakening is knowing that God wants for you what you want for your life. As others wake up, they will become pointers-of-the-Way or sharers of the Light, instructing as many as they can on the path to enlightenment. Enlightened beings will create many more enlightened beings until the human race as a whole is raised to a new level of higher consciousness. Your reading of this book may be serving as a catalyst to awakening. I hope so. The God In you will know when you have awakened and you will, almost automatically, begin to recreate awakened seekers along the way...no pedestal needed. There are many, many such individuals among us now, and we are recreating an awakening in others as this book is being read. And as for the religious leaders, some will choose to remain in their current state and some will choose to awaken to their elevated purpose...who is to say what choice they will make? But one thing is for sure, the worldwide awakening

IS HAPPENING and will inevitably continue...what will you

do?

My Personal Collective Consciousness Story

When I first began writing and publishing the messages that were being given to me, I was overcome with gladness, joy, and excitement. I had so many "aha!" moments that at times I could barely sleep. I had to get up in the middle of the night and write. The words flowed like water out of my soul and onto the pages. I was being inspired regarding subjects that were very different from the things that I grew up being told and had been taught to believe. Much of those things are the basis for my current spiritual awakening but many of those beliefs no longer served me so they needed to be replaced. As this transformation was taking place, I began to think genuinely about my family, my parents, my siblings, and my former church family, all of whom I love so deeply. I even thought heavily about some of my close friends who knew and believed as I had grown up believing. Somehow, I just knew that once the messages that God had purposed for me to deliver were published, that these people would immediately chalk me up as crazy, backslidden, blasphemous and demon-possessed, and disown me. These fears were mentally programmed scarecrows placed in my mind at an early age by religion and theological indoctrination. Yes, some of you are having the same thoughts as you awaken too. And for some, this might well be a possibility in your families. Of course, amid the joy and excitement there was this fear. Anyone who is to do something greater than themselves has this fear. So, I began to meditate and ask for complete boldness in the midst of fear to continue with the message in order to help someone else see that no matter their history, they still must go forward. I wrote my first book and submitted it for pre-publication. I ordered enough sample copies for my family so that I could make them aware of how "different" my message would be so that they would not be caught off-guard by its publication. No, the book did not contain any biblical references and not once did it mention the name of Jesus, not because I don't believe in them but because the message that I was given for that particular writing was to be passed on to everyone regardless of religious belief, spiritual orientation, or any other philosophical differences. The message has no boundaries because God told me that He has no boundaries. He is infinite.

And so, I met with my family at one of our annual family gatherings and gave out copies of my book for their perusal. I was especially concerned about how my father would feel, who is a prominent Bishop in our hometown deep within the Bible belt. I gave them time to read as much or as little as they wanted and then I waited...and this is how I know that (a) God lives in my family and (b) I had no need to fear...ever! No, this may not be their individual messages but because they love and support me, nothing changed.

Their love never faltered, but something very remarkable happened at the same meeting in 2013. As I began to talk to my family members individually, some of them began to share with me that they too were experiencing their own awakenings! As we began to compare notes, there was so much synchronicity in our stories! I would say that it was unbelievable, but it wasn't. It was confirmation that the divine spiritual foundation that we were given by my amazing parents was being expanded by The Source Of All Creation. The most amazing part of our conversations was that none of us had discussed what was happening to us with each other nor had we known that we were each expanding in the very same direction. Our awakenings began around the same time (near the end of 2011 for me) as well. Our talks were confirmation for me of our collective consciousness and encouragement to me to continue with this message of spiritual empowerment.

I and My Father Are One: My Journey To Waking Up

Having been born and reared in church, there aren't many types of services that I haven't seen. Still I wondered "why I needed to sit through all of that" and what had these people accomplished after years of these same types of services. I had no idea how all that I had learned would serve The Creator's purpose for me in my destiny. And of all that I had heard and memorized, I still had not become the student, for when the student is ready the teacher will appear. My teacher appeared in 2011 in the form of my own hunger for light following a series of self-created, eye-opening situations that turned out to be the catalyst for my seeking, awakening and enlightenment. I had been running from my purpose for a long time which created my misery. I wanted to be my highest self but even with all of the biblical verses I had memorized and all of my indoctrination, I had not had that enlightening, personal, oh-so-intimate experience with God that was to allow me to acknowledge the indwelling Spirit inside of me that would show me who I am. As with all humans, the inner prompting to acknowledge my God-ness remained consistent. I did not recognize it as God, I just thought that my life should be more than it was at that time. Why would I think that? Having come from small beginnings, God had given me a couple of beautiful homes, a smart, level-headed child, a couple of nice cars, a good government "job", and an amazing, hardworking, intelligent husband. So why wasn't this enough? Little did I realize that all of the money and possessions in the world would not be enough if I had not yet come to know and acknowledge who I am and whose I am...so I had to go back a few more years in my mind's eye...let's say 2006.

My journey to waking up seemed to take the express lane upon my mother's passing in 2006. She was the glue in my life and her death sparked a series of events that would be nothing short of God ordained. Up until that point I had been a social butterfly with limits. I was spiritual but still searching so I socialized with the best of them, dining, drinking and meeting new people constantly. After her passing, my drinking increased at a record pace and before I knew it, I was being arrested for more than one offense of driving while impaired. Determined not to have my story end there in that dark place, I didn't have to look far to see The Light of God's Love. It is as if The Light was patiently, lovingly, but still persistently waiting for my request to awaken and see it. When we are in a very dark room, even the smallest light seems so bright and it was in this space in my life that I began to re-member (put back together, reassemble) myself and my Source. The internalization of my spiritual awakening began to take form. I now know that experiences that we perceive as negative ones are always placed in our lives so that we may look again to the Source of our help so that we respond to these situations with our highest self and in our most awesome glory as images of God. So, I was prompted to quiet myself until led to do otherwise which turned into 5 months. I chose to yield to that prompting. I had little to no outside contact with friends and limited contact with family outside of my husband and our only child who lived at home with us. I chose to give myself over to study, fasting, and meditation to find my Self. It was in this timespan that God's voice from within me became prominent, recognizable, formidable, and dominant. He spoke to me about no one but me. He reaffirmed my identity to me in no uncertain terms and reaffirmed his UNCONDITIONAL love for me. Then, he began to speak to me through other people, places, things, circumstances, situations....he showed me what synchronicity really meant. He helped me understand that everything is according to His timing and that He allows me to choose the moments of His appearance in my life. I would not have known this had I been resigned to accept a life unfulfilled in purpose after such "earth shattering" experiences with the current legal system. As human beings, whenever we experience an event that is considered by society as both negative and permanent (losing a job, foreclosure, financial poverty, a run-in with the law, etc.), we label ourselves with these man made titles and see them as inhibitors to our purpose and success. But, alas! These are nothing more than words that humans attach to those who are too poor, too ignorant or just not in the right clique. If these titles are not accepted by us as individuals and are not allowed to play in the minds of each of us, then the titles are of no consequence when purpose steps in. And when we live in our purpose, those labels never hinder but only help us to deliver our message of love and acceptance. Today I am so grateful that The Source Of All Creation loved me enough to wake me up in this way and show me my worth and even push me into the journey towards the fullness of my highest potential and consciousness. Had it not been this way, I would not have sought Him so purely but would have spent the rest of my life finding ways to ignore and silence the voice of God in me causing those I could have helped in any way to remain in need, including me.

It was at this crossroads that I must make emphasis: I chose my path according to the promptings, but there were sure outcomes either way. I chose to hear and heed the voice of God in me, thus this writing among others as well as the manifested goodness that is my life today. However, had I chosen not to yield, resentment towards others who did yield would have been an eternal hell for me. At every success of another who yielded, I would have had to relive the hell of knowing that I did not listen to God. I would have died without realizing my full God Self. And so, in order to be in peaceful, powerful alignment with my inner God, I had to take heed and accept this love. In order to honor the God in me, I had to honor His voice and the feelings that follow His voice which comes from within me and say...YES!

The 10 Principles of Higher Consciousness

By Pauline Ritchie-Moore

1. The God in each of us is ALL POWERFUL.
2. Know that the God inside of each of us gives us unlimited power over our own lives. We are creators with God of our lives.
3. We are powerless over everyone and everything outside of us.
4. Know that our lives are in the hands of the Creator of the Universe, The Source of All Things.
5. The past is only to be rehearsed if it adds positive momentum to our forward motion. If not, the past is of no use or consequence. We know that our purpose is secure and sure or we would not have been given a desire for that purpose. The will of The Creator is that we have what we will.
6. Know that there is no "good" nor "bad", no guilt or shame, no ugly or unlovable here, no Greek nor Jew, no male nor female, no bond nor free. There is only love and light in everything and every situation so long as we seek to recognize it.
7. Know that we are perfect, acceptable and loved unconditionally at all times by the One Who Created Us. He is in us and we are in Him.
8. Know that we are to extend the same love and acceptability to all others in the Universe that has been extended to us.
9. Know that our mistakes are but an indicator of areas of opportunity for further growth and self-

love, if we only acknowledge this and seize these wonderful occasions.

10. Know that God is always with us, in us, around us, above us, below us, and never leaves us nor forsakes us because we are One with God.

www.ingramcontent.com/pod-product-compliance
Lightning Source LLC
Chambersburg PA
CBHW071149090426
42736CB00012B/2274